DOWNLAND HERITAGE

East Sussex through the eyes of an artist

FIRLE PLACE

EDWIN WILKINSON

S.B. Publications

First published in 2008 by S. B. Publications
Tel: 01323 893498
Email: sbpublications@tiscali.co.uk
www.sbpublications.co.uk

ISBN 978-185770-3399

Designed and Typeset by EH Graphics (01273) 515527

Front cover: *Plough and Harrow, Belle Tout Lighthouse, Charleston Manor and the Sussex Ox*
Title page: *Firle Place.*
Back cover: *The Sarsen Stone.*

CONTENTS

INTRODUCTION

Stretching from Eastbourne to Chichester, the South Downs present a beautiful back-drop to many Sussex villages and coastal scenes, their presence affecting weather and agriculture alike and, in turn, the social customs and way of life for those whose good fortune is to live in proximity to 'our blunt, bow-headed, whale-backed Downs', as Kipling called them.

Mountains are challenging, moorlands can be daunting, but the Downs are bracing and embracing, especially here in their eastern reaches on which this presentation of drawings concentrates, and which has long given me delight to walk and explore.

> 'The great hills of the South Country
> They stand along the sea;
> And it is there walking in the high woods
> That I would wish to be'.

Hilaire Belloc's expression will resonate with many who love walking the Downs and in doing so find renewal of body, mind and spirit, occasionally perhaps, staying to reflect and praise in one of those 'Little, lost, Down churches (which) praise the Lord who made the hills' (Kipling).

Coastal vistas and pleasant Downs inevitably draw admirers, and they, with fortunate local residents, can find social and physical refreshing at the inns and similar places in the area. Perhaps Hilaire Belloc's thoughts included them in writing, 'And the men that were boys when I was a boy shall sit and drink with me'.

There must be a wealth of experience and knowledge among those whose dwellings lie in the embrace of the Downs. From cottage and thatch to manorial elegance, the residents have achieved what Belloc hoped for,

> If I ever became a rich man,
> Or if I ever grow to be old,
> I will build a house with deep thatch
> To shelter me from the cold,
> And there shall the Sussex songs be sung
> And the story of Sussex told.

Admiration of 'the little Down churches', the inns and manorial residences, with their varied architectural and historical interest, motivated me to draw some of them for this publication. Not least, my love of the Downs in which most of these places are set, provided the greatest incentive to my endeavours! I echo Kipling's words loudly,

> 'God gives all men all earth to love,
> But since man's heart is small,

Ordains, for each, one spot shall prove
Beloved over all.
Each to his choice, and I rejoice
The lot has fallen to me
In a fair ground - in a fair ground -
Yea! Sussex by the sea!'

Edwin Wilkinson

ACKNOWLEDGEMENTS

With gratitude for their interest and permission to include material in this publication:

Mr & Mrs Hume - The Lamb Inn
Mr & Mrs Stacy-Marks - Folkington Manor
The late Paul and Mrs G Foulkes-Halbard - Filching Manor
The Proprietors - The Tiger Inn
Des, Paul and Pat - The Plough & Harrow
Mr & Mrs Lewis - the Rose Cottage Inn
The Eastbourne and District Preservation Society
William Shawcross Esq. - Friston Place
Lord & Lady Hampden - Glynde Place
Lord Gage - Firle Place
Clergy and Churchwardens of the Parish Churches
Mrs Rosalind Hodge for Friston Windmill
Mr & Mrs Roberts - Belle Tout Lighthouse
Mr & Mrs Kandiah - Charleston Manor
Nigel McKenzie - The Hungry Monk Restaurant
The Manager & Staff - Charleston Farmhouse
Mr & Mrs Pritchard - The Sussex Ox
Librarians at Eastbourne Central, Willingdon, and Polegate Libraries.

A particular word of thanks to Mrs Audrey Langley for occasional information gathering and assistance in preparing the text for the publishers, also to my wife, Joan, for her interest and constant provisions of sustenance throughout my endeavours.

Not least to Lindsay Woods of SB Publications for her advice and guidance.

THE LAMB INN

Leaving Eastbourne, westward, on the A259 the road climbs steadily towards the Downs. The Lamb Inn stands next to the impressive Parish Church of St. Mary the Virgin, both buildings obviously older than any in the immediate area which is still known as the Old Town. Writing about the origins of The Lamb, once known by pilgrims as 'The Holy Lamb', the nineteenth century historian Rev W Bugden comments, 'It may well be the site of the house granted to the Rector of St. Mary's about the year 1240, which is described as being next to the churchyard at Burne'. On request, visitors to The Lamb may be shown the rib-groined vaulting, with its rose boss, part of the original twelfth century building incorporated as the cellars in the sixteenth century renovations and extensions.

As the largest public building in Eastbourne, until the nineteenth century, its spacious facilities accommodated many social and civic events of the town. In addition the rapid increase in coach travel, from the seventeenth century onwards, saw the establishment of The Lamb Inn as a reputable staging post on the Brighton - Hastings route.

During the Napoleonic threat large numbers of military personnel encamped in the area, and especially on the Downs above The Lamb, the Inn becoming their focal point for balls and parties in the Long Room, as well as evenings of entertainment by theatrical groups and aspiring artistes.

Prior to 1606 the Inn was in the tenure of the Manor of Eastbourne - Gildredge, but from then until the mid-nineteenth century it was in private ownership. The present owners, Harvey & Sons of Lewes, carried out careful restoration work in 1912, also after the severe fire-damage of 1952.

THE LAMB INN, OLD TOWN,
EASTBOURNE.

FOLKINGTON MANOR

One mile west of Polegate this nineteenth century Manor stands in large cultivated grounds amid luscious farmland in the lee of the South Downs' Long Barrow. The magnificent house was built in 1844 by the architect Don Thorne, and the impressive stable-block was added in 1889, built by Peter Dollar. On the west wall of the stables, near the entrance arch, the stone Coat of Arms, with its uncompromising motto 'Repel force with force' is believed to be that of Lt. Col. Sir Roland Gwynne, the owner of the manor when the stables were built.

At the gate-house entrance to the private grounds the Stacy-Marks family crest is displayed. The Ibex was initially adopted as the family crest by Henry Stacy-Marks, RA., in the nineteenth century, and succeeding generations of the family have retained the emblem.

THE 19TH CENTURY FOLKINGTON MANOR

ST. MARY THE VIRGIN, OLD TOWN, EASTBOURNE

Leading out of Eastbourne the A259 climbs westerly to the Downs. One mile out, in the Old Town area, St Mary's Church and the Lamb Inn stand together attractively exuding history and tradition. Extensive fourteenth century alterations to the original twelfth century church have determined the proportions of the building as it is today, along with the benefit of an effective nineteenth century restoration.

Under a stone-barrelled ceiling the fourteenth century font holds a prominent and traditional position near the west door in the base of the huge tower. The nave arches are supported by alternate round and hexagonal pillars, while the 'flattened' appearance of the thirteenth century chancel arch is emphasized by the sloping walls of the chancel, purposely built with a wider base.

The modern east window is pleasantly dominating with its composite depictions of the Annunciation, the visit of the Magi, the Last Supper, and the Crucifixion. Four angels each hold a shield bearing symbols associated with the Crucifixion. In the upper quatrefoil of the window symbols of the four gospel writers are shown.

The chancel itself is beautifully balanced by the north and south chapels graced by their stained-glass windows of St. Michael in the north chapel and the Resurrection theme in the south. The Resurrection theme is also used in Meg Lawrence's colourful Millennium Window in the north aisle with its interesting introduction of the pomegranate, an ancient symbol of life and immortality.

ST. MARY'S
EASTBOURNE, OLD TOWN.

Edwin Wilkinson. 2003

Adopted as a Christian symbol, the pomegranate is sometimes shown bursting open to reveal the many seeds specifically symbolizing Christ bursting open the tomb in the Resurrection, the many seeds also reminding of the corporate life of the church.

Screen, memorials, hatchments, stained-glass and much more, present a fascinating unity of praise. Visitor, leave yourself time to absorb it!

HUGH EASTON'S 'ST. MICHAEL'. EAST WINDOW, NORTH CHAPEL.

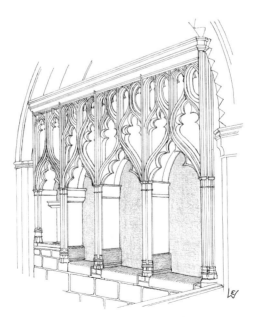

14TH CENTURY SEDILIA (CLERGY SEATS) & ROOD-LOFT PISCINA.

FOLKINGTON, ST.PETER

18TH CENT. PULPIT.

One mile west of Polegate turn off the A27 into Folkington Lane to the hamlet in the lee of the Downs. At the head of the lane the small thirteenth century church shares its wooded setting with the Old Rectory.

A weatherboarded bell-turret, added in the fifteenth century, pinnacles the flint nave and chancel. The organ and choir are situated at the west end of the nave, the organ having been given 'by Mary Earle Gwynne in deep thankfulness for the love that saved the life of her beloved son, Lt.Colonel Roland Vaughan Gwynne, in extreme danger in the battle of July 31st 1917 in Flanders'. The font and the restored box-pews survive from the fifteenth century.

A thirteenth century 'Devil's Door' in the north wall (see exterior drawing) was blocked up in the fifteenth century, probably when the north porch was built.

In the chancel the close-patterned stained glass of the lancet windows mellows the light. The church guide refers to an interesting, and perhaps unique, item to

FOLKINGTON, ST.PETER.

provide clerical comfort,' a medieval... globular silver vessel, which was filled with hot water and placed upon the altar so that the priest might warm his hands whilst celebrating Communion'. Alas, officiants cannot benefit by this comfort today, because this unusual and valuable item is kept in the bank.

The Gwynne and Thomas families feature prominently in the interior memorials.

17TH CENT. BOX PEWS.

(N.B) Devil's Door: Churches of Saxon, or early Norman origin, often had a north door which seemed to be used more selectively than as a general entrance, more in the nature of a door for clergy or church officials. A custom arose of opening this door at the point in the Service of Infant Baptism where the spirit of evil was exorcised from the child. The Verger, or attendant, would as quickly close the door again to prevent the evil spirit returning to re-enter the infant. By association the door began to be referred to as 'the Devil's Door'.

In the spiritual enlightenment of the Renaissance and Reformation it is conceivable that this custom became deplored as harmful superstition. At any rate, uniformly from that period, Devil's Doors began to be blocked up.

FRISTON, ST MARY THE VIRGIN

FRISTON'S TAPSELL GATE.

This small Early Norman church stands alongside the A259 at the junction with the Jevington Road, from which one gains the interesting aspect, as illustrated. An immediate feature is the Tapsell Gate at the entrance to the churchyard (see later note), and in the porch various 'graffiti', a medieval coffin slab, and remains of a water stoup. A heavy tie beam in the west of the nave at one time held the Holy Rood, the low Norman chancel and arch not being able to accommodate the figures. Miss Anne Gilbert of Birling Manor had the north transept built in the nineteenth century, providing additional seating and a place to house the impressive memorials to the Selwyn family, formerly of Friston Place. Notable also are the seventeenth century Selwyn brasses on the south wall of the nave. Two examples of modern stained glass are 'The Annunciation' by Marguerite Douglas Thompson in the north transept, and the chancel east end Millennium window 'The Ascension' by Jane Patterson.

A gem of a church evoking prayerfulness, for which there is the thoughtful provision of a devotional leaflet for visitors, presenting various prayers for personal needs.

MEDIEVAL COFFIN SLAB.

FRISTON, ST MARY THE VIRGIN.

12

FRISTON PLACE

FRISTON PLACE

The original building was erected in the early sixteenth century when Thomas Selwyn acquired the estate through marriage. Within the next century additions were made to the house on the west side, along with extensive interior alterations and renovations. Specific details of these can be found in John Farrant's 'Sussex Depicted'. Two dates, 1613 and 1634, with Selwyn family initials, are prominent above the east wing main entrance to the house, sited there from the earlier structure when the entire east wing was rebuilt later in the seventeenth century.

Throughout its various tenancies the house has been a 'working house' for the farmer/owners of the estate, particularly from 1754 when George Allfrey, followed by his son, established a reputation for excellent farming techniques. To this day the house retains its purpose and character as a private residence in the ownership of the Shawcross family, and notably Hartley William Lord Shawcross who was Chief Prosecutor at the Nuremberg Tribunal in 1945. A memorial stone to Lord and Lady Shawcross in St. Andrews churchyard, Jevington, describes him succinctly as 'Statesman, Patriarch and Yachtsman'.

A stepped Mounting Block, alongside the gateposts of the north-east entrance to the house garden, is a clear indication of the horse-riding tradition here, continued from the estate stables.

The flint and brick Wellhouse, in the north-east garden, is often referred to as the 'Donkey House', and retains the huge wooden donkey wheel, cogs and shafts, once used for drawing water from the well.

THE DONKEY HOUSE' FRISTON PLACE

FRISTON WINDMILL

Grateful acknowledgements are expressed to Rosalind Hodge for salvaging this lovely drawing of Friston Mill by a former local artist, and making it available for general interest, and appreciation, in this publication.

The illustration shows the third mill built on or near that site at Friston, unfortunately all three met disaster. The first, built at the beginning of the seventeenth century, was destroyed by fire in February 1761. The second windmill was over-powered by a severe gale in March 1826. A third mill and miller's cottage, was built by George Ashby in that same year of 1826. Anthony Hill's drawing shows the mill was standing close to, and on the north side, of St. Mary's, Friston.

Already in a state of some dereliction when the artist drew the mill, circa 1918, weathering and neglect took further toll until, in January 1926, a storm brought down the mill's body and sweeps leaving only the post and brick roundhouse as a forlorn remnant of what had been.

The last miller at Friston was William George Morris who was also Sexton and a choir-member of the nearby St. Mary's until his death in March 1922. A memorial tablet to William and his wife Jane can be seen in the south part of Friston churchyard close to the church porch.

Housing development now covers the area where the windmill once stood, its former existence reflected in the names of Windmill Lane and Windmill Close.

THE SARSEN STONE

This monument, its plaque fastened to a sandstone rock mounted on a double tiered flint-faced plinth, commemorates the acquiring of Crowlink Valley by the Seven Sisters Preservation Trust in 1926. Funds were raised by public donations and events, which included an aerial display by Sir Alan Cobham's team of flyers, finances from the Trust, and a generous donation from William Charles Campbell of Eastbourne. The aim of the purchase was to save the area from the developers and preserve it for public use. Happily, the aim was achieved and the monument testifies to it. The structure is sited near the Seven Sisters cliffs, and close to the South Downs Way, approximately one mile west of Birling Gap. In addition to its stated purpose the monument provides a welcome seat from which to admire the glorious coastal views.

The commemoration reads:-

> *This Sarsen Stone, presented by Viscount Gage of Firle, was erected by the Society of Sussex Downsmen in appreciation of the generosity of William Charles Campbell, Esq. to whose munificent donation to the Seven Sisters Preservation Fund was largely due the purchase of Crowlink Valley for the use and enjoyment of the nation 1926.*

THE SARSEN STONE

JEVINGTON, ST. ANDREW

Jevington village is situated just west of Eastbourne in luscious Downland country, the South Downs Way actually passes through St. Andrew's churchyard. The huge Saxon tower is the church's dominant feature along with the attractive nineteenth century porch, both were extensively renovated during 2005 and rededicated on the 6th November by the Bishop of Lewes.

The 'Anchor Crosses' on the roofs of porch, nave and chancel, symbolise the church's association with its patron saint, St. Andrew.

On the interior north wall of the nave a rare Saxon sculpture represents Christ's resurrection triumph over the beast of death. On the choir side of the much restored early English chancel arch, a memorial tablet is interesting for its unusual form of dating (see illustration). The seeming confusion is due to the change from the old Julian Calendar to the Gregorian system. In the Julian Calendar the year changed on the 25th March, but in the Gregorian Calendar on the 1st January. Since Nathanael Collier died on the 1st March, the Julian Calendar would reckon the year as 1691, but by the recently introduced Gregorian reckoning, the year would be 1692. The Gregorian system was not popular and took time to get established. It would appear the stonemason diplomatically included both figures so that the dating was accurate by either system.

St Andrew's, Jevington.

Look upwards to see the classic king-posts and hammer-beams supporting the Tudor wagon roof.

The attractive south nave windows portray the saints Andrew, Philip, George and John, while the east end window illustrates the Ascension, all are nineteenth century.

Modern richly coloured memorial windows in the north aisle beautifully depict St. Francis, St. Helena and St. Ambrose.

The wonderful Downland setting, and the church itself, provide a combined blessing not to be missed.

SAXON TOWER,
S.E. ASPECT.

THE SAXON SCULPTURE,
INTERIOR, NORTH WALL.

Near this place lyes y
body of
NAT. COLLIER
M.A.
late Rector of this
CHURCH
who dyed Mar:y firſt.
$169\frac{1}{2}$.

A REPRESENTATION OF THE
COLLIER MEMORIAL.

THE RECTOR, THE BUMBLE BEE
AND THE OFFERTORY BAG

It was Sunday morning, the first of May,
A wonderful, glorious, sunny day.
A hymn had been sung, the prayers had been said,
The wine was ready and also the bread,
When a droning, buzzing sound was heard,
Not the usual sound of a startled bird
But that of a Bumble Bee trying to find
His way round the altar to taste the wine.
We heard the Epistle and Gospel read,
And then the Creed was dutifully said,
And after that came hymn one-ninety-nine
And the blessed bee was still after the wine!
'Oh dear' thought the Rector, 'What a fag'
And then he remembered the Offertory Bag.
With one deft stroke he captured the bee
And folded the bag so that no one could see.
He placed it carefully on the sill
And went on with the Service reverently, till
The time came for all to come and receive
The Body and Blood for all who believe.

June spotted it first down by the rail
And tried to capture it but of no avail.
Then Brenda out of her pocket drew
A Kleenex tissue perfectly new.
She gave it to June who grabbed the bee
In front of the choir so all could see
And then raced down the aisle with blue robe flowing,
She flung open the door and still kept going.
There she released it and watched it soar
Into blossoms pink and flowers galore.
So pleased to be free, it went high in a line
To drink in the sunshine instead of the wine!

(Printed by kind permission of the author, Beryl Binnie, St. Andrew's Church, Jevington.)

FILCHING MANOR

Half a mile from Wannock, along the Jevington - Polegate road, the Manor is close to the road, nestling in the mouth of the narrow valley which winds up Combe Hill on the Downs. The Domesday Book refers to a Manor at Filching, and is tenanted at present by the Foulkes-Halbard family who trace their line to late Norman times, the Halbard family Arms being granted in 1302.

The present building is largely fifteenth century, set in secluded and pleasant grounds. The outbuildings, of more recent date, house an impressive museum of vintage vehicles and racing cars including Sir Malcolm Campbell's 'Bluebird' in which he broke the world land speed record in 1935, and the boat of the same name which captured the world water speed record in 1939. Aspiring speed enthusiasts can sharpen their skills on the Go-Kart track in the upper part of the grounds near the disused quarry.

FILCHING MANOR.
NR. JEVINGTON.

THE HUNGRY MONK RESTAURANT, JEVINGTON

The restaurant is well established in the fourteenth century building which originally comprised four separate dwellings to house monks who once served the monastery which was located near St. Andrew's Church. Situated in the centre of the village opposite Church Lane, the restaurant exudes an air of warm maturity, the combination of oak beams, panels, lounge sofas, original oil-paintings, soft lighting and fires, creates an intimate ambience.

In the late nineteen sixties Nigel and Sue McKenzie bought the building which was then the Monk's Rest Hotel, turned it into a restaurant and, retaining the monastic association, renamed it The Hungry Monk Restaurant. With its high-quality cuisine and intimate character the restaurant has gained wide acclaim and fame. An oval plaque on the front face of the building proudly presents the information, 'This is the home of Banoffi Pie, born 1972. One of the best loved puddings in the world'.

Banoffi Pie is the creation of chefs Nigel McKenzie and Ian Dowding. Its unique ingredient was the condensed milk cooked to form a soft toffee. Cream, caster sugar and coffee were whipped to a thick smooth cream. Based in a short-pastry flan the toffee was layered with sliced banana and thick coffee cream then sprinkled with coffee. Thus was born the world-famous pudding and, in a moment of inspired imagination, named and served by the chefs as 'Banoffi Pie'.

THE HUNGRY MONK
RESTAURANT, JEVINGTON

EAST DEAN, ST. SIMON & ST. JUDE

Situated on the lower south side of East Dean village, the flint-stone church appears neat and petite from the south aspect. In contrast, the north side is dominated by the huge Norman tower, which retains portions of its Saxon origin. Through the Tapsell gate and fifteenth century porch into the church, the appearance is of care and preservation. The organ pipes impressively housed in the king-post rafters of the nave ceiling. A twentieth century extension to the west end of the nave has provided a pleasing apse baptistry in which

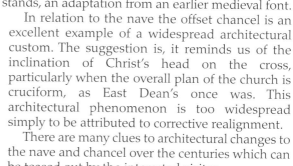

East Dean, St. Simon & St. Jude

the nineteenth century font stands, an adaptation from an earlier medieval font.

In relation to the nave the offset chancel is an excellent example of a widespread architectural custom. The suggestion is, it reminds us of the inclination of Christ's head on the cross, particularly when the overall plan of the church is cruciform, as East Dean's once was. This architectural phenomenon is too widespread simply to be attributed to corrective realignment.

There are many clues to architectural changes to the nave and chancel over the centuries which can be teased out by the interested visitor.

The churchwardens of 1623 presented the fine pulpit and sounding board reflecting the recovery of the Church's commission to preach and teach the Scriptures.

THE TIGER INN, EAST DEAN

The A259 Eastbourne Road separates the older section of the village from the extensive development to the north. In the older, south side, of East Dean the Tiger Inn can be found in the attractive grassy square which is surrounded by flint-faced cottages. Within the square a War Memorial stands central to the whole. The Inn is a popular venue for locals and visitors alike. In the summer especially, hikers find the outdoor tables pleasantly accommodating in sampling the fare at The Tiger.

Dating from the twelfth century the building has been an inn for much of that time, and is now in the ownership of the Davies-Gilbert Estate. At one time a smugglers' tunnel led from the inn to a nearby house. How did it come to be called 'The Tiger Inn'? The Rev. A. A. Evans, Vicar of Friston 1908-29, and local historian, suggests that the inn may have been so named in deference to the once powerful and locally resident family of de Dene whose heraldic Coat of Arms included a leopard, as did that of the later Bardolf family of East Dean. Within the same period the Medley family of Friston Place actually featured a tiger in their family crest. Those who have visited the inn may have pondered whether the symbol on the inn's sign board is that of a tiger or a leopard. Basically it has to be a leopard, but the adopted name 'Tiger' fits well enough.

THE TIGER INN,
EAST DEAN.

THE LONG MAN OF WILMINGTON

A splendid viewing-point has been provided at the head of the village where the road bends towards Litlington. 'The Long Man is one of the most impressive mysteries in Britain. It is the largest representation of the human figure in Western Europe being 235 feet long, yet surprisingly its origins remain obscure. The mysterious guardian of the South Downs has baffled archaeologists and historians for hundreds of years'. (Sussex Archaeological Society).

Similar 'Long Man' images are associated with Celtic and Norse traditions, usually portrayed with rake and scythe rather than staffs. Roman artefacts bearing similar images, but with spears instead of staffs, have strengthened the idea that the Giant was a warrior or war-god, and it has been discovered that at one time the giant's head was helmeted. There is no evidence that the monks of

THE LONG MAN OF WILMINGTON

the former nearby Priory originated the image. The meaning and purpose behind the Giant's existence remains as deep a mystery as ever, and some would say, 'All the better for that'!

WILLINGDON, ST. MARY THE VIRGIN.

THE PELICAN
LECTERN.

A REREDOS
ANGEL.

WILLINGDON, ST. MARY THE VIRGIN

Situated in Church Street, close to the A22, the thirteenth century tower is the oldest part of the building, attached to the west end of the fourteenth century north aisle and nave. A blocked doorway to an earlier building is a curious feature in the exterior west wall.

Dominant interior features are the wide Gothic chancel arch, the rood screen and rood, the screened north side Ratton Chapel, and the west gallery and organ.

Memorial windows reflect wartime influences. Near the pulpit the St. Paul window is an expression of thanksgiving by Mr. & Mrs. Strange for deliverance 'from the arrow that flieth by day' (Psalm 91 v.5); while the nearby War Memorial window beautifully portrays servicemen from Willingdon receiving the sacrament of Christ's redeeming love. The birth, death and Ascension of Jesus, 'The True Vine', are exquisitely represented. The south side window depicting Mary's visit to Elizabeth is also a thank-offering for the deliverance of the church, though damaged by bombs, during the 1939/45 war. The seventeenth century east end window remarkably survived without sustaining war damage and depicts Christ in glory, Richard of Chichester and St. Wilfrid. Fascinating details of these and the upper windows are worth noting in the Church Guide.

The Pelican Lectern shows the parent bird feeding her chicks with her own blood from her breast, a symbolic reminder of Christ's life-giving sacrifice.

The fourteenth century square font with panelled stem is topped by a modern baroque-style cover. There are interesting memorials, especially to the Parkers of Ratton and, connected with their family, Freeman Freeman-Thomas became Lord Willingdon, Governor of Canada and Viceroy of India. Baptized in St. Mary's and at one time its churchwarden, he died in 1941 and is buried in Westminster Abbey.

THE DUTCH-GABLED FORMER
POLICE STATION, WILLINGDON.
(OPPOSITE THE CHURCH)

WILMINGTON, ST. MARY & ST. PETER

Situated on the high ground at the head of the village, the Norman church is approached past the ancient Yew, older than the church itself. Beyond are the remains of the twelfth century Priory from which the church originated.

An association of thought with the Yew Tree inspired Paul San Casciani's design of the church's west end Millennium Window. The sectional rings of the Yew become the radiant circles in the window, symbolising the divine intelligence permeating the universe. Brilliantly coloured interspersed 'bubbles' suggest the vitality of the Spirit illuminating matter. Key to this theme is the incorporated text from the apocryphal gospels and attributed to Christ, 'Raise the stone and thou wilt find me, cleave the wood and I am there'. When lit by the evening sunlight this millennium window positively radiates brilliance.

The Flemish 'Butterfly Window', formerly in the north transept, depicting six butterflies, three moths and a bee around the figure of St. Peter, perished in an arson attack in July 2002. The restoration programme included moving the organ to the west end, effectively incorporating the north transept in the general area for worshippers. Happily a replacement window captures the same 'bee and butterfly' theme embraced by the phoenix.

The monks from the Priory at one time used the chancel for worship, hence the stone seats (Sedilia) on the north and south sides. The small stone carving placed high in the north wall of the chancel in 1948 is thought to be a Norman Madonna. The Jacobean Pulpit and Sounding board is outstanding, reflecting the spirit of renaissance and biblical learning. The square font on a central stem is fourteenth century.

WILMINGTON, ST. MARY & ST. PETER

REMAINS OF 12TH CENTURY PRIORY.

LULLINGTON: THE CHURCH OF THE GOOD SHEPHERD

LULLINGTON,
THE CHURCH OF THE GOOD SHEPHERD

High on the Downs the church can be approached from the Wilmington-Litlington road along a sign-posted leafy pathway between cottages and allotment gardens. Alternatively a longer footpath can be followed from Alfriston, over the Cuckmere River via the White Bridge.

Not always as small as this, the church is the restored chancel of a fourteenth century church said to have been destroyed by fire in the seventeenth century. Even so, from 1356 there is a list of Vicars of Lullington until 1927 when the church was united with the benefice of Alfriston.

Added in the nineteenth century restoration, the weather-boarded bell turret houses a single bell, cast in 1806. The area of the church's former nave and porch were revealed by excavations in 1965-6. A facsimile of the detailed plan of the excavations, from the Sussex Archaeological Collections, is displayed in the church.

With basic furnishings of Communion Table, Lectern, Font, Reading Desk, Harmonium, and seating for twenty three people, Services are held once a month during the summer season. Formerly without a known dedication its present, very appropriate, 'Church of the Good Shepherd' was officially adopted in September of the millennium year.

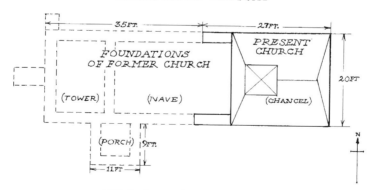

LULLINGTON CHURCH

APPROXIMATE DIMENSIONS OF
THE ORIGINAL CHURCH.

LITLINGTON, ST. MICHAEL THE ARCHANGEL

This Norman, flint-faced, church with its attractive bell turret, stands alongside the Wilmington Road and close to the South Downs Way in the Cuckmere Valley. Traces of the thirteenth century sundial remain on the wall of the porch. Interestingly, near the porch stands the memorial to Charles Joseph L. A. Trobe Esq. CB., the first Lieutenant Governor of the colony of Victoria, Australia, who at one time lived in the Litlington parish.

Within the chancel is a double fifteenth century Sedilia (clergy seating), and a thirteenth century piscina (stone sink for washing Communion Vessels).

The north and south lancet windows in the chancel are Norman, with glass possibly thirteenth century.

Behind the sixteenth century Font, with its Jacobean cover, is the low door in the nave north wall opening to a spiral staircase leading to the belfry. The belfry houses three bells one of which was cast as far back as 1450 by William Chamberlain at the Whitechapel Bell Foundry.

N.B. John Henry Parker's Glossary of Architectural Terms gives the information: 'The use of bells in churches for the purpose of assembling the congregation appears to have been introduced into England at a very early period, and are supposed to have had their origin at Nola (whence 'nola', "a bell") in Campania (whence 'campana' -

LITLINGTON, ST MICHAEL THE ARCHANGEL.

campanology). The illumination of St. Aethelwold's Benedictional shows that they were in use in the tenth century. As early as A.D. 674 Bede mentions the 'hearing the well-known sound of a bell'.

ONE OF A TRIO

16ᵀᴴ CENTURY FONT & BELFRY DOORWAY.

ALCISTON CHURCH (No Dedication)

Approximately one mile west of the Alfriston roundabout turn off the A27 into the hamlet of Alciston where the cul-de-sac is headed by the church, Alciston Court, and the farm. Old street lamps and a fenced pathway across the farm field make an attractive approach to the church. To the right, at Court House Farm, there is a medieval dovecote and monastic tithe barn.

The Normans replaced the Saxon church but recent excavations near the east wall uncovered a part of its foundations. In the fifteenth century the chancel was altered and shortened; evidence of the alterations can still be traced in the walls. Following modern trends the chancel is strikingly open and unfurnished.

Crossed-section beams supporting the west end bell-turret make an interesting feature in the king-post roofing. Two fourteenth century bells are housed in the turret, one is dedicated to St.Agatha, the patron saint of bell founders.

Plain glass in all the windows adds to the light openness of the whole interior enriched by the warm pine of the modern pews.

ARNOLD MACHIN'S TERRACOTTA ANGEL.

ALCISTON CHURCH, (DEDICATION UNKNOWN.)

THE MONASTIC TITHE BARN,
COURT HOUSE FARM.

THE ROSE COTTAGE INN, ALCISTON

The hamlet of Alciston lies on the south side of the A27 approximately one mile west of the Alfriston roundabout. Nestling immediately under the Downs, The Rose Cottage Inn is prominent in the varied dwellings of the hamlet.

The sixteenth century building, which once housed the local store, has received modern adaptation to turn it into a Pub with, more recently, excellent restaurant facilities. The beamed bar area is cosy with tables and open fireplace, its character enhanced by Jasper the African Grey Parrot, limited but lively in his cage on the bar. Harveys of Lewes provide most of the ale, while ploughman's lunches and special dishes are also available. The restaurant has a smaller section within what was the old cottage. Its low, bowed ceiling and beams justify it being called 'The Snug'. The larger area of the restaurant lies at the front of the building in the recently extended and delightfully refurnished section, light and welcoming and, again, an open fireplace.

A comprehensive restaurant menu and wine list is available in the evening with an emphasis on the use of local produce. Outdoor tables are also at one's disposal.

An ancient custom of 'Skipping' is maintained at the Inn on Good Fridays when dancers gather to enact the ceremony. The custom has uncertain origins and its history is chequered, but it seems to have been revived locally after the Second World War. It is said the ceremony may have developed from a primitive belief that stamping on the ground encouraged the crops to grow. Another idea links the ceremony to the repairing of fishermen's ropes and gear. Either way, the event is colourful and interesting in front of the Inn in the beautiful setting of the Downs.

THE ROSE COTTAGE INN,
ALCISTON.

BERWICK, ST. MICHAEL & ALL ANGELS

Turn off the A27 just west of the Alfriston roundabout. From the car park near the vicarage follow the walled pathway to the church.

The Norman building, with the fourteenth century broach spire, owes much of its present character to two factors: The incumbency of the Rev. E. Boys Ellman who, during sixty years as Rector from 1846 - 1906, completely renovated the hitherto derelict building. Another factor was the Second World War which brought bomb damage to the building. On the initiative of the Bishop of Chichester (The Rt. Revd. George Bell) many of the stained-glass windows were replaced with clear glass. In addition the 'Bloomsbury Group' of artists, living at nearby Charleston Farmhouse, were commissioned to paint the murals which so effectively adorn the entire interior of the church, and were dedicated by Bishop Bell in October 1943. These works of Duncan Grant, Vanessa Bell and Quentin Bell are listed and explained in the excellent church guidebook.

THREE TIER MASONRY SAXON FONT.

When rebuilding the church the Normans left the Saxon font in its original position, virtually building it into the west wall structure. The church notes give information of a similar Font in St. Martin's, Canterbury, where King Ethelbert was baptized by Augustine in A.D. 597.

ST. MICHAEL & ALL ANGELS, BERWICK

THE PLOUGH AND HARROW, LITLINGTON

Situated in the luscious beauty of the Cuckmere Valley, within the hamlet of Litlington, the Plough & Harrow Inn provides an attractive venue for local people and visitors alike.

An astral 'plough' accompanies the agricultural plough and harrow on the inn's signboard. To good effect the present proprietor has added a real plough and harrow at the front of the building.

Last century's flint styled additions are sensitive to the surrounding environment, blending comfortably with the seventeenth century original part of the building. The extensions provided kitchen facilities also increasing the Lounge and Bar space. Good food and real ale are characteristics of this Free House.

A tabled garden at the rear affords additional pleasant surroundings for refreshments and the occasional Barbecue.

THE PLOUGH & HARROW, LITLINGTON.

THE SUSSEX OX

On the east side of the Cuckmere River, approximately one mile away from Alfriston, The Sussex Ox stands at the head of the hamlet, Milton Street, affording magnificent views of the Cuckmere valley and surrounding Downland.

Of late nineteenth century date the original brick building was used as a slaughter house and shop serving the community with meat, locally grown produce, and groceries until the Second World War. The huge influx of military personnel into the area probably influenced the introduction of beer being sold in the shop. Along with the social and economic changes of the times, the building itself changed to that of a Public House under the name of The Royal Oak.

Extensive structural alterations in the early 1970s also brought a change of name to The Sussex Ox, but the place has continued to be noted for its provisions of fine ale and good food in its unrivalled Downland setting.

The Sussex Ox

Edwin Wilkinson

THE CUCKMERE WHITE HORSE

On the west side of the Cuckmere Valley a horse has been fashioned by cutting away the turf and shrub to reveal the white chalk beneath. The impressive image is best seen from the road between Charleston Manor and Litlington. Those who have walked to the viewing point on High and Over will have stood, perhaps unaware, just above the horse's mane.

The origins of the horse are uncertain. Some believe the original horse was cut as a memorial to a girl who was unsaddled, and killed in the fall, when her horse bolted down the hillside. Prior to the present horse it is said a horse had been cut by the tenants of the Frog Firle Farm to commemorate the Coronation of Queen Victoria. That effigy gradually disappeared as turf and shrub reclaimed the area. The present ninety foot horse was cut into the chalk in 1924 by Messrs Ade, Bovis and Hobbs, local residents who, apparently, worked by moonlight to give their fellow neighbours a morning surprise, which it must surely have done!

Recently Frog Firle Farm and the White Horse have come into the care of the National Trust who, with the assistance of East Sussex County Council, have maintained the Chalk Horse as an admirable visual image in this already beautiful valley.

THE CHALK HORSE ON HINDOVER HILL

BELLE TOUT LIGHTHOUSE

Belle Tout (Good View) overlooks the cliffs from Beachy Head to Birling Gap, once notoriously dangerous to shipping. Under those cliffs, at high tide, shipwrecked mariners were trapped with no way of escape. The Reverend Jonathan Darby, Vicar of East Dean and Friston 1706-1726, conducted many of the unfortunate's funerals. Driven by concern the Vicar caused a series of caves to be hewn in the sheer cliffs at least fifteen feet above high water and accessed by steps. Darby himself hewed out a cave able to be entered from the top of the cliff and used to house a light. From these rescue 'Darby Holes' came the first local attempt to provide a warning facility for shipping.

A century later the local MP and landowner 'mad Jack Fuller', provided a small lantern-bearing wooden structure on Belle Tout, replaced in 1834 by the stone building housing one of the first flashing lights and visible for twenty miles. Unfortunately, recurring mists and fog limited the effectiveness of the cliff-top lighthouse, prompting its decommissioning in 1899 and replacement with the Sovereign Lighthouse in 1902 sited at the base of Beachy Head cliff.

Since 1923 Belle Tout Lighthouse has been in private ownership, visited by King George V and Queen Mary in 1935. During the Second World War stray shells from a nearby gunnery range rendered the building battered and derelict. Fortunately from 1955 under Dr. & Mrs. Cullinan, and successive owners, the building has been completely restored as an attractive residence. This distinctive landmark has been location for many film companies, notably in 1986 by the BBC for Fay Weldon's 'Life and Loves of a She-Devil'. In 1998 a massive and unexpected cliff fall left the lighthouse approximately six meters from the edge of the cliff! Thanks to the endeavours of Mr. & Mrs. Roberts, the then owners, and the brilliant engineering work by Pynford Engineering of Watford in March 1999, the entire building was hydraulically lifted and moved fifty-five feet away from the cliff. To compensate for the loss of height in the downhill move away from the edge of the cliff, concrete foundations were constructed to retain the former lantern-house altitude of the lighthouse. The move should preserve the building for generations to come.

CHARLESTON MANOR

Charleston Manor is situated on the east side of the Cuckmere Valley between Litlington and the Exceat corner. Trimmed yews line the long shingled drive leading to a triangle bounded by the Manor, Staff Cottages, and the Old Coach House. The Manor is a private house described by Nairn and Pevsner as 'the perfect house in the perfect setting'. The oldest part of the Manor is a rare example of Norman domestic architecture, probably once the Manor Hall including a chapel in the upper storey, evidenced by the two-light window at the north end with its five shafts and foliage capitals.

In its long line of owners, notably, was Roger de Leyburn who, in 1264 had become Warden of the Cinque Ports and held the Manor in 1293. A wing was added on the east side in the fifteenth century and a further wing in the eighteenth century. Spanning 177 feet is a double barn fronted by an expansive lawn presenting an idyllic setting for weddings and receptions, and currently licensed for such occasions.

CHARLESTON MANOR, EAST VIEW.

Edwin Wilkinson.

A medieval dovecote retains its centre post and revolving ladder-frame giving interior access to the nests. Approximately forty contented doves are presently nesting. Alongside the dovecote is a fig tree conveying its own pleasant symbolism of desired prosperity and well-being.

The Millennium sundial: A sculpted foliate Green Man, mounted on a panelled stone plinth forms the sundial. This ancient symbol represents the personification of nature's life force and fertility. The inscription reads; 'Peter and Julia Kandiah commissioned this sundial to mark the millennium. MM.

NORMAN
CHAPEL WINDOW.

THE MILLENNIUM SUNDIAL

MEDIEVAL DOVECOTE

SELMESTON, ST. MARY

The flint church with its typically Sussex bell-turret, stands proudly central to the ribbon development of Selmeston, five miles west of Polegate. Saxon origins are indicated by the circular churchyard, and an entry in the Domesday Book, 1086, confirms a church on the site. The original building has given place to much alteration and restoration through the centuries, but especially in 1867.

Richly coloured nineteenth century stained glass in the east window concentrates on the theme of the Crucifixion, while the south aisle windows portray the wonder of the Resurrection. A thirteenth century water stoup and Easter Sepulchre survive in the chancel, while the Credence Table (chancel south side) is supported by two beautifully carved stone angels, one playing a harp the other praying, an appropriate theme of prayer and praise.

Unusually, the hexagonal pillars supporting the south arcade are oak.

Various brass memorials show how our English language has changed over the centuries; e.g. the brass to Henry Rogers (south aisle) describes him as 'a painfvll preacher in this church two and thirty yeeres'. Not, of course, 'embarrassingly awkward', but one who 'painstakingly' prepared and delivered his subject. He died in 1639 but his memorial still testifies to his steadfast faith and dedication, 'expecting the Second coming of our Lord Jesus Christ, I did beleeve and therefore spake. Whereof I tavght I doe pertake'.

SELMESTON, ST. MARY.

THE ANN COX MEMORIAL *Situated in the floor close to the chancel, the black marble ledger stone bears the inscription: 'Ann, Widow of William Cox of Stanstead in the County of Kent, and daughter of Robert and Elizabeth Rochester. Died 1741, aged 57 years'. Facing the shield, the arms on the right are those of Ann's father, those on the left the paternal or granted arms of her husband. The three things arranged round the chevron may represent heraldic 'grenades'.*

(Acknowledgements to Melvyn G Jeremiah, CB, JP, Hon. Sec. to The Heraldry Society).

POLEGATE, ST. JOHN

The coming of the railway in 1846, and subsequent improved road links, gave impetus to the development of rural industries and housing around Polegate. To serve the steadily growing population St John's was built as a daughter church in what was then the parish of Hailsham. The Foundation Stone was laid in 1875 and the church opened for services in November 1876 to be consecrated in August 1878. Responding to the continued population increase in the area, Polegate became a separate parish, with St. John's its parish church, in 1937.

An attractive broach spire tops the north west tower and entrance to the church. Substantial roof beams and brick facing characterise the interior. Beyond the chancel arch the shallow chancel is clear, choir stalls and organ having been situated in the north transept. The Caen stone reredos has inlaid marble panels depicting geometric symbols of the Holy Trinity, each enclosing Greek monogram symbols relating to the person of Christ. In extension of the reredos four panels display the Ten Commandments, Apostles Creed, and Lord's Prayer. Above the reredos the Ascension is the theme of the beautiful east window. Both reredos and window were donated by the Diplock family in 1885 in memory of Sarah Matilda and Caleb Diplock. The nave windows are in clear glass, apart from that in the upper circle of the columned south window. On the south side of the chancel the once 'Vicar's Vestry' is now an open chapel.

St. John's, Polegate

Edwin Wilkinson

POLEGATE WINDMILL

This brick Tower Mill, standing forty-seven feet high, was built in 1817 for Joseph Seymour, a local miller, whose family owned and worked the mill for a century. In 1915 ownership passed to the Ovenden family who used it as a commercially viable wind-driven mill until 1943 when the fantail mechanism fell into disrepair and became unusable. Without this essential means of directing the cap and sails into the wind, the milling mechanism was then driven by electric power.

Gradually becoming commercially unviable, and mounting repairs needed, the Ovendens sold the mill in 1965 to the newly formed Eastbourne & District Preservation Society through whose Trust the mill has since been cared for and restored in stages, until at present it stands sound and complete, open to the public and an attractive landmark in the Willingdon-Polegate area.

The mill is located on the south side of the A2270 in the district of Willingdon, approached along a well-signed unsurfaced lane.

Through the extension of the Polegate civic boundary in 1939 its former title 'Willingdon Windmill' gave way to 'Polegate Windmill', its present designation until, perhaps, the boundary reverts!

POLEGATE WINDMILL.

St. Wilfrid's, Lower Willingdon.

LOWER WILLINGDON, ST. WILFRID

St Wilfrid's was built as a daughter church in the parish of St. John's, Polegate, dedicated on the 23rd. June 1962, to serve the rapidly expanding area of Lower Willingdon and Wannock. The church is situated in Broad Road opposite the Secondary School, with open views of the nearby Downs. The architects were Benz & Williams of Ringmer. Built largely with prefabricated materials it nevertheless blends well with the surrounding housing development. Pre-stressed reinforced concrete trusses, partial panelling, and clear glass windows throughout, provide clean modern lines in a light and bright interior, the whole contained under a single-span roof. The furnishings are simple. The Font, provided with the essential original furnishings, is a hand-beaten aluminium bowl with afrormosia cover supported by a wrought-iron tripod representing uplifted hands. The accompanying water-ewer is also handmade and aluminium.

The present church hall is Chris Boyce's enlargement of the original building and was dedicated by the Bishop of Lewes in 1990. The building contains offices, vestry, meeting-rooms, cloakrooms and WCs and an upstairs hall, making an attractive and effective unit for the benefit of the whole community. The adjoining Clergy House was built in 1964 and enlarged in 2002. Made a Conventional District under the Church of England scheme in 2003, it is reasonable to suppose that St. Wilfrid's might become a parish in its own right before long.

OVER THE HILLS AND FAR AWAY

I've been wandering all the day,
Over the hills and far away;
Through a valley just near the sea,
Where sheep bells played a melody;
Treading the turf where cowslips nod;
Watching the working oxen plod;
Seeking for flints in furrows brown;
Doddling over the open Down;
Meeting rabbits and flowers and trees,
Butterflies, birds and bumble-bees,
Thousands of creatures, each a friend,
Names and addresses without end;
No book tells all I saw today
Over the hills and far away'!

(Barclay Wills)

BARCLAY WILLS: 1877-1962

Downland historian and archaeologist, an illustrator of natural history with a particular interest in the life and customs of Downland Shepherds, recorded in the books of his authorship. He moved from London to Sussex in 1922 to follow his business interests, and respond to his increasing love of the Downlands.

Mr L. M. Bickerton, one time Curator of Worthing Museum, described Barclay Wills as, "...one of the most learned and endearing men Worthing has known".

MY SUSSEX BELL

The ancient sheep bell on the wall
Is stored with memories dear
To an old shepherd of the Downs
Who always loved to hear,
Among his other 'canisters',
A deep, far sounding call;
He listened for the mellow note
And thought it best of all.

For eighty years he knew the bell,
Since he was shepherd boy,
But long before those happy days
His father knew the joy
That it could give, and ever since
Succeeding ewes have borne
The favourite over Downland hills
Till now its rim is worn.

With drowsy hum of wandering bees
'Mid nodding harebells blue,
With whispers of the quaking grass,
And scent of thyme, which grew
Upon the little hill-side mounds,
Its ever welcome song
Was blended by the downland breeze
And gently borne along!

What countless grass-blades touched the bell,
With fingers soft and green!
What countless flowers, as it passed,
Have kissed its mouth, unseen!
So much there is I long to know
The iron tongue cannot tell,
And so I weave what thoughts I may
Around my Sussex bell.

(Barclay Wills)

THE CLERGY HOUSE, ALFRISTON

From the main street in the centre of the village turn down the lane alongside the United Reformed Church, and walk through to the grassy square. The Clergy House is evident, on the south side of the fine Parish Church, an attractive thatched and timber-framed early fourteenth century cottage.

The name, traditionally given to it, suggests the original purpose of the building was to house the clergy who, at that time, were probably serving the churches and parishes of Alciston, Alfriston and Lullington under the general care of Battle Abbey and its monks, though this is not certain. However, there is no doubt that the Clergy House is a fine example of a 'Wealden' house, and became the first property to be bought by The National Trust in 1896 for the princely sum of £10.

THE CLERGY HOUSE, ALFRISTON

WHITE BRIDGE, ALFRISTON

The lengthy White Bridge spans the Cuckmere River at the eastern edge of Alfriston, close to the parish church. Specifically a footbridge it is an essential and attractive asset to hikers following the South Downs Way, or tracking the Vanguard Way along the Cuckmere Valley. It also provides a convenient link for those wanting to walk from Alfriston to Lullington Church, or the Downs beyond, following the path by Great Meadow Barn.

Those who enjoy walking the Downs, and particularly the Cuckmere Valley, will have 'trodden the boards' of the bridge. Alongside the bridge on the Alfriston bank a mounted plaque informs: 'White Bridge Alfriston. Refurbishment of White Bridge, and improvements to its approaches, funded by East Sussex County Council Rights of Way & Countryside Management, with contributions from The Countryside Agency, and Sustrans Ltd., in partnership with The Millennium Commission. Reopened by Alfriston Parish Council on 3rd November 2000'. Well done everyone!

THE WHITE BRIDGE, ALFRISTON.

THE STAR INN, ALFRISTON

In the centre of the village, itself in the heart of the East Downs, the thirteenth century Star Inn is an obvious attraction. Built as a hostelry it became well known and used by the local community and travellers alike, particularly by pilgrims during the medieval period when the Inn was administered by the monks from Battle Abbey and Michelham Priory. Until the sixteenth century the Inn had the fuller appellation 'The Star of Bethlehem'. The Star has long been in private ownership and remains so today.

Guests are accommodated in en suite bedrooms, the bar and lounge are situated in the original part of the building, as is the first floor meeting room. A twentieth century addition houses the fittingly designed plaster and beam restaurant. The whole ambience of the building lends itself to offering 'its guests a unique blend of oak beams, open fires, intimate atmosphere, and traditional hospitality'.

The Sanctuary Post in the bar area is a link with the past monastic privilege of sanctuary. Anyone who touched it could claim sanctuary against the rigours of the law or religious persecution. Apparently smugglers used this facility to great effect!

Another curio is the Red Lion Figurehead which stands in a corner of the front exterior of the Inn. Reputedly it is a fifteenth century figurehead from a Dutch Warship which sank in the Channel. Eventually it washed ashore as flotsam in Cuckmere Haven where it was found by smugglers who brought it to Alfriston. Conceivably the vivid effigy provided an unmistakable marker for the 'night owls'.

THE STAR INN,
ALFRISTON.

Edwin Wilkinson.

CHARLESTON FARMHOUSE

Midway between the villages of Firle and Berwick along the A27, a clear sign indicates the entrance to the long drive leading to the seventeenth century Charleston Farmhouse. In 1916 the artists Vanessa Bell and Duncan Grant, influenced by the Post-impressionists, turned the place into a focal point and sanctuary for their colourful decorative style of painting.

The household attracted other artists, writers and intellectuals known as 'Bloomsbury'. Outstanding were Clive Bell, David Garnett, Maynard Keynes, Virginia and Leonard Woolf, E.M. Forster, Lytton Strachey and Roger Fry. Over the years Vanessa and Duncan's exuberant designs were transferred to all parts of the house and furnishings, while the garden, with its delightful ponds and willow, was endowed with numerous statues.

On certain days there are guided tours through the house, on other days the visitor can range and muse at leisure through this unusual but fascinating treasure trove of art. The exhibition gallery, tea room, and shop, provide additional interest with books, ceramics and textiles, presenting and propagating the colourful medium of the Bloomsbury artists.

Bloomsbury themes are presented in drama, talks, art, and literary works at the Charleston Festival held annually in May.

The nearby Berwick Parish Church holds many fine examples of murals and panels produced by the Bloomsbury artists in more traditional style.

CHARLESTON
FARMHOUSE

ALFRISTON, ST. ANDREW

At the United Reformed Chapel, on Alfriston's main street, turn down and follow the pathway which opens onto the village green. The large fourteenth century St. Andrew's Church is immediately obvious with its impressive tower and shingle broach spire central to the nave, transepts and chancel. The church's dimensions contributed to its unofficial title 'Cathedral of the Downs'.

Entrance is by the west door and porch, under the west gallery, formerly a 'minstrel gallery'. Tall arches support the central tower, traditional king-post beams hold the roofs of the nave, chancel and transepts. Nineteenth century pine pews have replaced the earlier box pews, adding to the feeling of spaciousness within.

Apart from the ancient glass in the north transept, depicting St. Alphege, all the stained glass is nineteenth or twentieth century, and includes examples of Kempe-cum-Tower glass in the south transept. Plaster figures of St. Alphege, St. Andrew, and a panel illustrating Christ calling St. Andrew, were placed in the Easter Sepulchre (Sanctuary north side), having been saved from the obtruding stone reredos, removed in 1987 to leave the entire east window unobstructed.

Stone seats for clergy (Sedilia), and a Piscina (stone washbowl) adorn the south wall of the Sanctuary. The north and south transepts each have a Piscina, indicating they were used as chapels.

The architectural design of the central tower

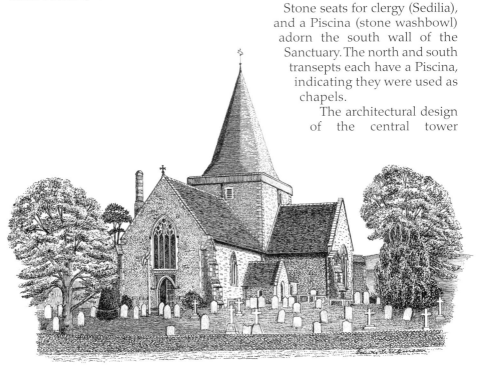

ALFRISTON, ST. ANDREW.

precludes provision of a 'ringers' chamber', consequently the ringers stand in the body of the church to ring the bells. Of the extant six bells the tenor is the oldest, cast at the end of the fourteenth century. A disused bell of 1587 is on display near the font.

JESUS CALLS ANDREW THE FISHERMAN.
(A THREE-DIMENSIONAL PLASTER PLAQUE)

GLYNDE PLACE

Glynde Place and estate is situated on the northern edge of Glynde alongside the minor road which rises through the village. Caen stone and Sussex flint characterise the mansion built in 1569 by William Morley, an ironmaster. Built around a courtyard, now Lady Hampden's garden, the west wing was the front of the house. When the Bishop of Durham, the Rt. Revd. Richard Trevor, succeeded the Morley's in the mid-eighteenth century, he immediately undertook an extensive building programme.

He had the east wing enhanced, also building the brick and flint stable block with its distinctive clock tower. Two Welsh dragons

were added to the east gate pillars, virtually completing the bishop's aim of converting the front of the house from west to east to overlook the expansive and pleasant grounds of the estate.

Visitor information indicates Glynde Place is the family home of Viscount and Viscountess Hampden. On given days during June to September inclusive, individuals and groups can tour the house and five acre gardens by arrangement. 'Portraits, furniture, silver, embroidery, books and a collection of Italian Masters, testify to four hundred years of family life'. The tea-room and gift shop add to the visitor's pleasure.

WELSH DRAGONS GUARD THE EAST GATE.

GLYNDE PLACE, EAST WING.

18TH CENTURY CLOCK TOWER
& STABLE BLOCK.

GLYNDE, ST. MARY THE VIRGIN

The classic Georgian church, at the upper end of the village, stands next to Glynde Place, looking to Mount Caburn and an impressive Downland vista.

A church stood on this site from the twelfth century until 1763 when Richard Trevor, Bishop of Durham and at that time owner of Glynde Place, ordered the dilapidated church to be replaced, resulting in the building we see today. The few degrees northerly realignment of the new building complemented the stable block and clock tower of Glynde Place, added about the same time. Only the bell and a silver chalice survive from the earlier church. The interior is also classic Georgian, the chancel area and nave contained under a single roof span, a concave ceiling with light rococo moulding, box pews, a once 'three decker' pulpit, a west gallery and organ.

Unusually, and effectively, the interior walls are covered with hessian bearing a fleur-de-lys pattern, thanks to a 1983 restoration programme by the then Brighton Polytechnic.

An elaborately carved walnut screen, by Kempe, erected in 1894 was removed in 1983, so preserving the clean Georgian architecture of the whole. Formerly on the screen, the pelican symbol, with emblems of the Passion, was placed on the fascia of the gallery. Of the seven superb stained-glass windows five are by Kempe (1894) incorporating rare Flemish panels. Hatchments to Henry Otway, Lord Dacre (1853), and Thomas Hay of Glyndebourne (1786), adorn the north and south walls respectively.

GROUND PLANS OF
ORIGINAL AND PRESENT CHURCHES

(Reproduced by kind permission)

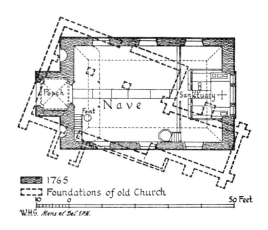

THE PELICAN SHIELD Pecking its breast to bring blood to feed its young, the Pelican's action became a symbol of Christ's own self-giving to win life for us. The four circles represent the Four Gospels enclosing emblems of the whipping and crucifixion of Jesus. The spears, the crown of thorns, the sign 'Jesus of Nazareth, King of the Jews', are all portrayed on the cross. The whole set in a circle of eternity.

THE PELICAN SHIELD

GLYNDE, ST. MARY THE VIRGIN.

FIRLE PLACE

Henry VIII's Vice-chamberlain, Sir John Gage, enlarged an existing building here at Firle to make a significant family home. Elizabethan renovations, expansive eighteenth century additions, particularly to the north west frontage, along with Georgian and Victorian influences throughout, have provided a hugely impressive house and home for the continuous line of the Gage family from Tudor times to the present 8th Viscount Lord Gage and his family.

On visiting days, tourist connoisseurs have a chance to appreciate an array of portraits and landscape paintings, including such eminent artists as Holbein, Joshua Reynolds and Van Dyke. Classical porcelain, furniture and furnishings are also to be admired.

Near the rear entrance to the house stands a rather rare disused flint and brick nineteenth century Gas House where ammonia and lime were fed with water to produce acetylene gas stored in the tower. Under pressure, the gas was then piped to the house to provide effective lighting by its intense white flame. An interesting piece of industrial architecture.

The magnificent house, stables and farm-buildings of the estate, are set in gardened parkland on the wooded Downland slopes under Firle Beacon, and appear to cradle the village of West Firle.

FIRLE PLACE

THE GAS HOUSE.

WEST FIRLE, ST. PETER

St. Peter's is situated on the upper side of the village, close to Firle Place. Approached by the west drive the impressive thirteenth century tower is seen to advantage. Entry to the church is by the fifteenth century south porch.

The succession of Vicars at the church goes back to William the Conqueror's time, according to the list in the vestry. The church, as we see it today, is largely thirteenth and fourteenth century, replacing an earlier, smaller building of which the north door is a survivor.

Clerestory windows help to lighten the nave, while the window above the altar in the south chapel, depicting the Crucifixion, contains original fourteenth century glass. A richly-coloured John Piper window (1985), graces the sixteenth century north chapel as a memorial to the Sixth Viscount Gage, its theme is based upon the Tree of Life, musical instruments and animals symbolise God's praise in life's vitality. Within the chapel there are impressive and varied memorials to the Gage family, from Sir John Gage (1556) to the present time.

At the east end of the north aisle the renowned brasses, including the 'Bolney Brass', bear testimony to the sixteenth century merger of the Bolney and Gage families.

There is so much of historical and architectural interest to be gleaned here, in a church intrinsically linked with the Gage family of Firle Place.

WEST FIRLE, ST. PETER.

TARRING NEVILLE, ST. MARY

This twelfth century church on the south west slopes of the Downs overlooks the River Ouse and Newhaven. A Norman building with an Early English tower, the walls are heavily rendered, apart from the nave's south wall and east end of the chancel, which are knapped flint. The fourteenth century porch is rendered also. Traces of a Scratch Dial can be seen on a window reveal on the south wall of the nave. King-post beams support the roof, and the use of plain glass, in most of the windows, adds significant light to the interior. A remarkable feature is the font, which has been incorporated as part of the 'Good Shepherd' window at the west of the nave. The Font is built partly into the wall with its basin positioned where the window-sill would normally be!

In the chancel a low window on the south side enabled lepers to observe the Services, particularly the consecration of the bread and wine at Communion, hence such windows becoming known as 'Leper Windows'. On the north wall of the Sanctuary is a rare open orifice (best seen from the exterior) by means of which lepers, or the sick in times of plague, could actually receive an administration of the Sacrament.

The church's long heritage is reflected in the list of Rectors dating back to 1288. A piece of heritage, recently stolen from the church, was the iron chest reputedly salvaged from a ship of the Spanish Armada in 1588.

St. Mary's was restored by the Victorians then, to mark the millennium, by English Heritage and donations from the local people. Pastorally, the church is linked with St. Leonard's in nearby Denton.

THE 14TH C. WALL-TIED FONT.

TARRING NEVILLE, ST. MARY.

WEST DEAN, ALL SAINTS

West Dean Village nestles in a secluded cul-de-sac off the lower reaches of the Cuckmere Valley. The church's heavily buttressed Norman tower is impressive, capped with a half-hipped, clay-tiled, spire. The design of the cap is said to be unique in Sussex, and its appearance has been likened to a monk's hood.

A well-preserved Norman arch, beneath the tower, graces the west-end interior of the nave. During extensive renovations in 1963 a small window was uncovered in the nave north wall confirming the church's Saxon origins. The rood screen which separated nave and chancel, was removed in the mid-nineteenth century, to be followed in 1977 by the removal of the choir pews to leave a completely open and spacious chancel.

The Victorian East Window depicts the Crucifixion and, on either side of the window the Ten Commandments are displayed, while on the south side of the chancel is a fine example of a shell-shaped piscina, used at one time for washing the communion vessels.

Those whose interest inclines to memorials will be able to admire the angel figures on the early seventeenth century memorial to William Thomas and his wife and, perhaps, gain a little practice of Latin! Maurice Theodore Lalbrance, killed in September 1916 while on active service in France, is remembered in a window depicting St. Maurice, martyred in 286 AD, and St. Theodore, Archbishop

THE OLD PARSONAGE

of Canterbury 690 AD. The artist Sir Oswald Birley is commemorated by the bronze bust crafted by Clare Sheridan and unveiled by Lady Churchill in 1958. Sir Oswald lived for a time at the nearby Charleston Manor. A commemorative bronze bust of John Anderson, first Viscount Waverley, was sculpted by Jacob Einstein and unveiled by Prime Minister, Harold Macmillan, in April 1960. The Viscount was a resident in West Dean and is buried in the churchyard. Prestigious connections with a prestigious church in a prestigious setting. This is certainly a place well worth visiting.

The thirteenth century former parsonage flanks the lanterned entrance to the churchyard.

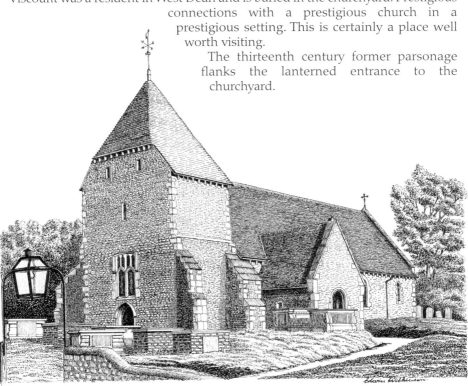

ALL SAINTS, WEST DEAN.

BISHOPSTONE, ST. ANDREW

At the western edge of Seaford the road to Bishopstone climbs up the valley towards the Downs. Prominent on a higher ridge, under Beacon Hill, the relatively high walls and narrow nave of the church are typical Saxon, while the impressive, staged tower is entirely Norman.

A Saxon sundial, inscribed 'Eadric', is evident above the Norman entrance to the Saxon porch, prompting the question, 'Who was Eadric?'. Could he have been a bishop benefactor of the church for, until the seventeenth century, bishops of Chichester occasionally resided at the nearby manor. When the Normans added the north aisle they sensibly followed the pitch of the main roof to the low north wall, now heavily buttressed to prevent 'spread'. Counter to prevailing custom the north 'devil's door' has been retained. The ribbed vaulted ceiling gives special character to the east end Sanctuary, while in the lower chamber of the west tower a rare coffin slab is worthy of attention, (see the illustration). A continuous rope forming three circles represents the Holy Trinity: the drinking doves an early Christian symbol of the life-giving Holy Spirit, especially in baptism; Christ is the Lamb of the Agnus Dei; the beflowered Calvary Cross represents the Church's living witness to the redemptive work of the Cross.

Early Christian art often combined these symbols of the dove, the Lamb, and the cross, and here they are combined on this twelfth century coffin-slab.

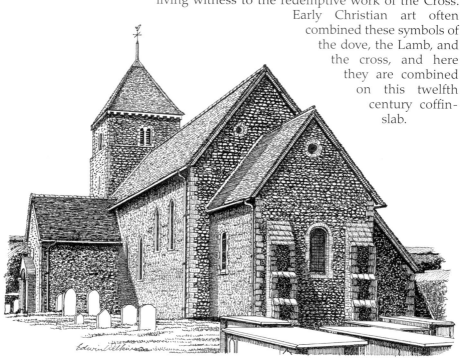

St. Andrew, Bishopstone.

Situated next to the church the 'Eadric House' Almshouses bear the date 1856 and the motto over the doorway, 'Lord bend our wills to thine'. Now, under a charitable trust, the Almshouses are still used for the benefit of parishioners.

12ᵀᴴ CENTURY COFFIN SLAB

SAXON SUNDIAL & NORMAN DOORWAY.

19ᵀᴴ CENTURY ALMSHOUSES, 'EADRIC HOUSE'.